SWIMMING WITH A HUNDRED YEAR OLD SNAPPING TURTLE

Swimming With
A Hundred Year Old
Snapping Turtle

𝒫OEMS BY FREYA MANFRED

Red Dragonfly Press
Minnesota
2008

ISBN 978-1-890193-76-8

Printed in the United States of America
by BookMobile

Cover drawing by Bly Pope
Title page drawing by Rowan Pope

Typeset in Amethyst Pro and Alexander Quill (for tittle)
both designed by Canadian type design Jim Rimmer
Rimmer Type Foundry

Published by Red Dragonfly Press
press-in-residence at the Anderson Center
P. O. Box 406
Red Wing, MN 55066
www.reddragonflypress.org

CONTENTS

3. *One True Thing*

For my sons, Rowan and Bly

To A Young Artist

My poems are written by a spirit on a stone,
and there are many tellers, many stories, and many stones,
in honor of our braided paths and solitary ways.

Now, at sunset, I'm called to where water merges with land and sky,
where an eagle drops from a tall pine, dips her beak into darkening waves,
rises with a flapping silver fish, and flies away.

I wish you work that weaves a spell, and love,
and breath – uncounted, irretrievable, sacred breath,
flying from its cage of bones – eagle-falling, fish-rising, free.

1. Swimming With A Hundred Year Old Snapping Turtle

Fields that mean more than fields,
more than life, and more than death, too.

Edna O'Brien, *Wild Decembers*

Swimming With A Hundred Year Old
    Snapping Turtle

I spy his head above the waves,
big as a man's fist, black eyes peering at me,
until he dives into darker, deeper water.
Yesterday I saw him a foot from my outstretched hand,
already tilting his great domed shell away.
Ribbons of green moss rippled behind him,
growing along the ridge of his back
and down his long reptilian tail.
He swims in everything he knows,
and what he knows is never forgotten.
Wisely, he fears me as if I were the Plague,
which I am, sick unto death, swimming
to heal myself in his primeval sea.

Rain On Water

All afternoon rain streams down on the lake
until a break in the black clouds
draws me out of the house
into the rocking waves.

I dive through layers of darkness, layers of light,
and when I come up for air,
the sky echoes the underwater world,
speaking the unspoken,

not a warning, or god-like, "It shall be!" –
more a wind-driven, earth-embracing *word* –
and I swim to meet it,
from the lake into the sky.

Next to this the body is nothing,
and the mind less than the body,
and only the country of the heart
is equal to what I know.

Swimming In The Rain

I swim in the rain, alone
in the gray place
where lake and sky meet.
Thousands of bright drops
drum the waves,
and disappear,
leaving radiant silver bubbles,
which burst
as more drops take their place.

I'm glad no one is with me,
surrounded by the numberless lamps
of this liquid city I have never seen,
whose residents turn on, turn off,
their beckoning lights —
signaling the stars.

The Owl Cries At Night

The owl cries at night,
and I imagine her wide gold eyes
and feathered ears tuned
to the trembling woods and waters,
seeing and hearing what
I will never see or hear:
a red fox with one bloody paw,
a hunch-backed rabbit running,
sand grains grating on the shore,
a brown leaf crackling
under a brown mouse foot.

With so much to learn,
I could stop writing forever,
and still live well.

Eye Of Loon

A loon swims toward me underwater
in a lake that lies eighty feet deep,
and I freeze,
as if he were some savage, ancient predator.

We hang,
in clear indigo, in time and space.

His blood red eye meets mine
and looks through me,
past me —
into the dreadful eye of the universe.

Death Of A Hundred Year Old
Snapping Turtle

I haven't seen him all summer,
though he's trolled past our dock every day for years,
surviving speed boat drivers, jet-ski jockeys,
and fishermen, drunk or sober.

Is he nursing an injury?
Did he die of old age?
I feel strangely lost, abandoned,
without his dark shadow in the lake's scattered light.

But, look! Near shore, a small black head
pops above the waves, a tiny replica of his.
And at my gasp of joy, she drops from sight.

Grief

Twelve white whooping cranes
their black beaks shining
float like spirits on the ice-blue lake.

And yet a bed of tears lies under me.
I cannot raise my eyes to the winter sky
as the cranes lift, one by one, and fly away.

Dreams

Choose a safe place to dive under, and open your eyes
to bottomless staircases winding up and down, to underwater rivers
which may at any moment break through the floorboards, uproot the bed,
rushing in to quench your thirst for the living and dying gods and demons
sleeping in the smallest marsh marigold, or in the unpredictable
sad and joyous words of people you trust, or hope to trust.

This much is true: I married my husband after dreaming of a black egg
pierced by white lightning, and eased into mothering with dreams of valleys
ripe with trees. I kept the smooth blue stone that rose to meet my hands
when I flew frightened and alone across the earth, seeking myself.
I saw the eye in the mountain turn into a breast as I soared closer
to whoever I was – whoever we all were – before you and I were born.

Rescuing The Children

Almost all of mine were rescued, in dream after dream,
when I moved next door to the house where I was born.
The willful two year old crawled under the fence to freedom,
joined by curious three, sensitive four, bold five, careful six,
and seven, a seeker, with faraway eyes. Twelve escaped too,
forever working on her chores like a little coal miner, while
lanky ten jumped hand in hand with eight from their perch
in a friendly tree. Even pimply thirteen, who grew four inches
in a year, clawed her way to safety, bleeding a ribbon of blood;
and sad, lumbering fifteen was joined by nine, perhaps the
strongest, since she waited to free herself until most of the
rest had flown. Eleven and fourteen stayed behind, too
fearful to leave. But everyone celebrates the fact that nine
can fly. Nor will she lose this art, until death takes us all.

Honey For The Hive

I feel flatness in things once curved,
and see dead-eyeball white where I once saw color.
I can't smell the breath of pines in the woods
or hear water rushing over sand and stones.
Is this what it means to be crazy?
Am I bleeding to death?

You know the rhythm I've fallen out of touch with,
the spark we strike when we wake tuned to the planet's turning,
echoing the moon's path as it rises from the arms of the sea,
over the shoulders of mountains, across unfolding fields –
how faithfully it lights the garlands of rivers and seas
connecting the dark and drifting continents.

Babes in the womb do not lie still. We swim.
We circle. We open and close our fists.
We eat our mothers. We are born dying.
We follow the reliable disintegration
of the beasts and bees who come seeking us
to gather fresh meat, and honey for the hive.

Fear

I fear not being able to walk,
choking to death, and watching others
weep with pain when they won't let me help.

I fear an old friend's voice over the phone,
rich and deep,
saying he no longer wants to live.

Fear is a thirst for solid ground,
a cave and a fire,
with a way in, and a way out.

Fear is not always old, but it's always new.
When old, it can be ignored,
like the midnight keening in the houses of the sane.

When new, it's nameless,
something about to happen –
not death, but all I can imagine.

Fear leaves and returns.
There are no words to keep it away.
If only there were words.

The Fantasy Of Speaking And Being Heard

I don't like to lie about how little I care,
how slowly I react to people dying, even those I love,
even the fervent midnight certainty that I will die.
I could say our culture has dulled me to waves of violence,
buildings burning, dead bodies in the flooded streets,
corpses of children flung about as dogs fling dying rabbits
or cats torture mice they don't intend to eat. I could blame
my sick son, my lonely mother, or a husband I can't trust.
Or maybe it's my age, my health, my need to talk with someone
who can't wait to hear my story, someone not paid by the hour
to cash my jagged feelings, someone who whispers,
"Let me take your hand and hold it to my heart.
Let me say I love you, because I hear you speak."

Taos Mountain

The walk to the foot of the mountain
took days,
though its blue chest and shoulders
seemed so close
from a distance,
its peak like an old man's face
with high cheekbones,
eyes full of tears.

A week passed in the piñon
and the pine,
while I waded shallow red rivers
to cool my feet.
On the last day
the old man's face grew fuller,
angry, then comical,
then peaceful as a baby's.

When I finally stood on a boulder
at the bottom of the mountain
and looked up – up – up –
the face had grown into
a fiery jumble of rock,
above, below, and all around.

Plain earth,
the true story.

The Deer Who Won't Go Away

To save him, I stopped traffic with waving arms
and sent him galloping
across the highway to our woods,
where he waited in the lilacs by the front door,
sniffing the wind and studying me.

Later, he legged silently up behind me
as I weeded the garden, and stood
three feet from my outstretched fingers,
more composed and curious
than any deer I've ever seen.

I am drawn outside, again and again,
toward his gentle assertion.
He won't permit my touch,
but gazes at me with the brown eyes of a lover.

His breathing alters my breath
until I'm no longer aware of myself,
or of anything –
separate from his gaze.

Stars

What matters most? It's a foolish question because I'm hanging on,
just like you. No, I'm past hanging on. It's after midnight and I'm falling
toward four a.m., the best time for ghosts, terror, and lost hopes.

No one says anything of significance to me. I don't care if the President's
a two year old, and the Vice President's four. I don't care if you're
cashing in your stocks or building homes for the homeless.

I was a caring person. I would make soup and grow you many flowers.
I would enter your world, my hands open to catch your tears,
my lips on your lips in case we both went deaf and blind.

But I don't care about your birthday, or Christmas, or lover's lane,
or even you, not as much as I pretend. Ah, I was about to say,
"I don't care about the stars" – but I had to stop my pen.

Sometimes, out in the silent black Wisconsin countryside
I glance up and see everything that's not on earth, glowing, pulsing,
each star so close to the next and yet so far away.

Oh, the stars. In lines and curves, with fainter, more mysterious
designs beyond, and again, beyond. The longer I look, the more I see,
and the more I see, the deeper the universe grows.

I have a long way to go, and I'm starting now –
out in the silent black Wisconsin countryside.

Swimming Into Winter

As winter approaches
I often swim without a life guard
or even a friend watching from the shore,
returning to stones, sand,
lake weed, fish, the sky.

I know it's foolish to stay so long
in October water, but I'm swimming
out of my daily life, out of myself,
losing heat to the source,
my heart to the universe,

until the soft lake water
holds me back from nothing.

2. Just Like A Woman

It's strange that our love of Beauty should lead us to hell.
I caught one glimpse of you, and a moment later
My house and books were all thrown into the fire."

Robert Bly, "Monet's Haystacks"

[These poems arise from conversations with others about their marriages, and from reflections on my thirty year marriage to my beloved husband, Tom Pope. Thus, many voices speak.]

What could we have said, that we did not?

Everything that made our story more true.

What could we have given, that we did not?

Only what we couldn't give to ourselves.

What can we say or do, now?

A Soldier To Her Husband

Last night my dreams were arduous marches, worse because
none of us knew why we had to leave our homes in mid-winter,
why we had no shoes, or why my husband fell behind the rest.

I went back to look for him, and though we only heard each other's
voices in the dark, I urged him to push ahead of me across fields
of falling snow. We passed many hooded strangers with guns

on their shoulders, who didn't care if we lived or died. I wanted
to run forward to find our sons as we'd left them, broad-shouldered,
faces bright, carrying our grandchildren on their backs.

Torn between saving or risking myself, I would have preferred
a more cowardly route. I never saw our sons again, though word
passed down the line that they were well. When I woke, shuddering,

I couldn't remember if you were with us, husband, though I searched
every ravine and frozen pond for your face. But *someone* was with me –
I can still sense his presence among the marchers, advancing toward

no place we knew or would ever know. Yes, I felt your shadow,
my love, as you wrapped me in a blanket of reverie, and handed me
water in a cup, which I was permitted to drink *only* because you existed –

though I am no longer certain of your shape, and can no longer hear
the sound of your consoling breath.

Decisions Born Of Small Gestures

When my husband is away,
I miss him less than I used to.
He comes. He goes.
But I no longer stand dazed
and bereft in our bedroom,
unable to sleep or dream.

Sometimes I stroll behind him,
and wonder who he is.
I'm sure of nothing, except
that I don't know what love is.
How is it when he beckons me with one finger –
my whole body follows?

I buy a black rain coat and spy on her from behind a newspaper.
I recognize her from the secret snapshots she sent my husband,
a trim blond with bird-claw fingers. I crash her fancy house party,
drink red wine, and smile mysteriously. Her husband tosses down
a scotch and winks at me. Now that I've penetrated their lives,
what next? Shall I get even with her by throwing twenty years
of love letters at her husband's feet? Torture him for no reason,
as I was tortured? Why do I feel so ashamed? Where is my joy?
How will this end? I have no answer. My husband says he'll
love me forever, yet here I stand, one foot out the door —
incognito, clandestine, in my black rain coat.

Once

I won't make love with him one more time.
When I look into his sea-green eyes I no longer believe
there's a safe landing to our incandescent free-fall.
I no longer have the courage to fly where evening
shadows swallow and release us to dawn,
where we rest in each other's arms and remember
how each life entwines with the other – how roots
tunnel faster than dreams, than hope, than thought or light,
and there is no time and we never die.
But how would I understand something so true
if I hadn't made love with him, once?

One Dark Snore

I no longer feel like a wife,
a monster, or a labyrinth.
I'm going to live with many
men now, or none at all.
A few men told me I was
lovely, but I rarely felt it.
They said the same to my
friends. The best men *are*
friends. I thank the universe
they exist. But, if you marry,
make sure you can survive
five grunts, four growls,
three sighs, two precious tears,
and one dark snore at midnight,
that tears away the veils.

Why I Can't Stay Married

I've never gone nuts
and I don't want to start now.

If I go crazy, my husband will let them lock me up.
It's even possible he's driving me in that direction.

I can't be stuck in one of those scary asylums you see in movies
where people wring their hands and can't get out.

It's bad enough to weep and moan here – if I cry *there*,
the doctors will inject me with drugs

for the crime of having strong feelings –
the crime of becoming a loon.

And we all know how crazy those loons sound!
They wail, laugh, yodel and hoot

for four reasons known to science:
to connect with other loons over long distances,

to speak to their family,
to express alarm,

and to warn of intruders –
especially man.

Kind Young Stranger

Lost in L.A.
I had two quarters to call my family
but couldn't remember the name of our motel.
A kind young stranger drove me back
in his green Fiat.
He was earnest, but teasing.
I felt old enough to be his mother.
I wondered whether he was in love
with some wonderful girl,
but when he turned his freckled face
toward me and spoke
there was nowhere else I wanted to be.
In the motel he chatted with my husband
while I tried to give him money for gas –
but all he wanted was a kiss,
which he took with one finger under my chin,
gentle and firm
as sorrow.

The Nemesis Speaks

> My wife is my nemesis.
> — overheard at a party

The wife says: "My husband doesn't want me around so I sip
too much wine to keep from choking him. I act as if I care
about what he's saying, and cry, 'You're right!' when I know
he's wrong, predictably looking out for himself when I need
someone to look out for me. Sometimes I wish he was dead
so I could stop feeling such a fraud. To calm myself, I imagine
I'm cradled by invisible arms while I seek some deeper truth.
Truth: that thing he cannot speak when it's all I ask of him."

Vanishing Point

The moment arrives when you say,
"I don't dislike this man,
but how did I marry him?"
Something about his wintry voice,
the way he can't or won't show his face,
and how small and alone you feel
out here on earth's curve,
driving day and night,
never reaching a destination,
until you realize you're running parallel to him,
and you'll never meet.

Betrayal And The Moon

She was betrayed by a man who said he'd die
rather than lie to her,
yet made a living out of lying, so as not to die.

The first betrayal was like blood on the moon,
an ancient birthmark, never removed.
The second, a lunar eclipse: black circle in a halo of fire.

The third time he lied, the moon loomed so close
there was nothing solid left to stand on, so she swam
toward the silver light pouring through the watery sky.

How could she resist the moon's pull,
blooming each month with a scarred and broken face.
Moon – grown so curiously fond of her eyes!

Man, Woman, Moon

Drink in the alien eyes of this wild one
you don't want to lose,
who doesn't want to lose you.
Make sure he can find his way home in the dark,
when he forgets who he is, or you forget,
because even after thirty years
you don't know what he's thinking
when he stares out the window at the snow
falling in veils past the moon –
the same moon you've been watching
every month since you were born.

A Man Must

A man must push the door open
and pull aside the drapes
after I've drunk his wine.
He must make no sound,
and take my hand softly,
and not look into my eyes
but gaze fondly out the window
at the golden trumpet flowers.
This, before I can hold him
in the curve of my thigh,
and stroke his hair,
and turn the page
and read to the end,
and know more about him
than he knows about himself.

Stranger

One of us, my love, will see the other dead,
mouth open like a baby's in sleep, cold hands
curved into claws, as if all these years an unseen,
unspoken, unwilling, unloving alien inhabited our bodies,
turned only and always toward itself, denying laughter or love:
beyond sickness or sadness, beyond horror or hope –
the one we glimpsed as children when our mother's arms
fell away from us, or our father closed the door forever.
At last this outsider inside us emerges – and the one we were
surrenders to the stranger we've become.

Tonight As We Walk By The Sea

Salt water from the sea mixes with fresh water
flowing from underground caves whose great black wombs
are lit by stars before they start their journey toward the sky.

We dream the galaxy was born in earth's waters
and wade eagerly into the waves with the anemone, the seaweed,
the starfish, the fragrant weeping grains of sand.

The wild surf rises out of the sound of its own singing
and travels toward us, wings spread like an ancient Pterodactyl,
until we run for our lives against a wall of water

rushing back toward the sea. But we never forget
how we were welcomed into the universe: surprised, overtaken,
nearly obliterated, by something within us and without.

3. One True Thing

Look inward at the story only...

Philip Roth, *Exit Ghost*

One True Thing

She reaches a point where she wants to say one true thing:

Her best friend cannot bring himself to love his adopted daughter.
Her neighbor is so stricken by her solitary childhood
that she can't let her son play alone, in peace.

Her boss won't spend a penny of millions to help
his hard-working grandkids with college.

As for her small role in all of this,
she is torn between loving everyone she knows
and wishing she'd never met any of them.

To stay alive, she swims in blue-green lakes and red wine,
pretends she's four or four hundred, reads books,
and imagines herself dying.

She fears she has no family or friends who will take her in.
No one who will join her in the place she needs to go
to heal and understand –

the place where she will hear one true thing.

Touching Bottom

> Are we frightened of the great, delicate spaces
> Under the waters...?
>> James Wright, "A Visit To The Earth"

The list of things I no longer care about grows long,
though when I recall myself as a girl of twenty, swooning
in the springtime Shakespeare class of James Wright,
what mattered most to me then has not changed:
a good conversation with a man neither old nor young,
lost nor found, only a poet, becoming, on a journey.
Can we manage that, without New York sarcasm creeping
into our voices, without bland Midwestern superiority,
or West Coast faith in one right path, like lemmings to the sea?
Can we let each other finish a story without interruption,
speak our greatest fears and hopes without a moral,
until we're not unlike two friendly dogs on a wild romp,
with no plans except our muddy, barking acquiescence
to each other's strange, rich, ancient, singing world?

I have so many stories to tell.
My mother listens to my stories and cries,
"That would make a marvelous novel!"
When she dies, who will listen to my stories?
Maybe I can tell them to myself
while I walk along the country roads.
I can't remember the last time I told a good story
to my friends, though they've told me a few doozies.
Maybe it's time to look for new friends.
My stories want to get on down the road
and it's my job to follow.
I may love your story more than I love you,
and when you listen to my story
you give birth to my song.

Five Rough Old Oaks

When I was one, five rough old oaks
outside our country home
became my second family.
I nibbled their dry, bitter bark
and let it cloak my tongue.
I crawled across their spreading roots
and looked up, branch after branch,
until the tops could not be seen –
only imagined, waving with the seeking,
sighing, never-forgetting winds
of all the lands I'd never seen.
How lucky I was to learn so young
to taste and trust a world held up by trees.

Thunder

53

The thunder gave thirst to the earth!
Jerome Crow Dog

When I was a child and I heard
gruff thunder above the house,
and great gusts of wind swept across
our yard, and a thirsty silence speared
straight up from every grass blade,
I ran outside naked to feel the soothing,
stabbing needles on my skin.

Now that I'm old I still long to feel
the waters of the world descending
in galaxies of drops like melting stars,
traveling toward everyone alive
with an ardent, terrible voice.

First Friend

Once, where shadows fell black and twisted
on the forest floor, he stepped, dark-skinned
and slender out of the mossy side of a great
red oak. Did he tell me his name was *Friend*,
or did I say it? Thirsty, he drank my water.
Lonesome, he laughed at my jokes. Solitary,
he sometimes chose a separate path. We met
every morning after breakfast to make plans:
to wake with the sun and fall asleep with the
moon, each in a swaying tree; to hate adults
who said we shouldn't play in distant swamps
and dangerous rivers. What did they know
of freedom, unless they knew too much?

When I was seven, Friend gently slipped
away without either of us saying goodbye.
My new pals, like my dear husband, were
easy to talk with, since Friend and I had shared
a lilac house for years. But now, as a loon
cries lonely from the lake, I wonder who will
travel with me to the other place – the place
Friend came from? Come back, Friend!
If you do, we'll never leave each other again.
And if you don't, I'll find my way to you.

Best Friend

When I was ten my best friend was Diane Pond.
She could bake a cake from scratch. Sewed her
own clothes. Swung from the hay loft on a rope.
Skated miles on frozen streams. Undressed to
show me her breasts just starting to swell, and
asked me to touch them while she touched mine.
She was the only girl in first grade taller than me
but far more lovely, with Snow White's ebony
hair and white skin, and strong broad shoulders
like mine, which our mothers bemoaned.
We strode the halls side by side until fifth grade,
when teachers put her in another class because
she wasn't "school smart." She invited me to her
Presbyterian Sunday School to learn about Jesus,
and didn't get mad when I said that I was bored.

Diane wouldn't leave me, and she didn't lie.
Every word we sang or whispered in the sultry
summer woods was the tomboy truth, until her
family moved away, and I promised to write
but never sent one letter. Five years later I heard
she'd married a boy with black hair when she
and he were barely eighteen and gave birth to
a baby girl who died, but a year later they had
a second daughter and gave her the same name.
Not my name – but Rachel, from the *Bible*.

I don't know why I didn't write her. Our joy
was wild, skin to skin and skin to sky. Not
something you want to lose when you're left by
yourself, young-girl bones still growing toward
a universe of cold stars, and you can't find the
courage to tell your first best friend goodbye.

Leon

Leon had twelve children and lived in Shakopee
where the great pacer, Dan Patch, was born.
He and his wife got by on his salary as a gardener
for the wealthy doctor next door. When I stalked
him through corn stalks and asparagus bushes,
he'd pretend not to notice until I jumped out, "Boo!"
Then he'd chuckle, stop hoeing or raking, and put
one foot up on a stump to roll a smoke. Through
half-closed, flint-black eyes, he'd tease me.
Was I sharp-eyed enough to spy the old mother
rabbit in the lettuce patch? The red-tailed hawk,
dropping to its prey? The half-buried agate in the
sand? Did I want a ride on the Great Council Oak,
where Leon's Grandfathers used to meet with other
tribes to smoke the Sacred Pipe? Leon lifted me
onto the lowest branch and warned me not to break
its skin, tender and wrinkled as an elephant's hide.
I stroked the velvet, listening leaves, their ears as
large as his, while he sang to the sky-swimming oak.

The Pain You Have To Learn

The healing herb itself gets sick.
Jerome Crow Dog

Giving birth, I escaped into my breath,
echoing everything on earth –
in, and out,
summoning and sending away –
until there was no difference,
except I was small
and earth was large.
This is what animals know:
every stone, water drop, and wind
sighs in unison
with a woman giving birth –

and giving birth,
I fell toward falling,
until our sons,
our sons,
our beautiful sons were born.

To The Children

Go outside. Since nature is dying,
take care of your small part of the garden we have left.
Smell the earth: inhale sun on dirt, wind on leaves, rain on wood.
Dig a hole. Plant a seed. Water, and watch it grow.

    Oh, why do I have to cry out with such cliches!

Just do what I say, over and over,
until you hold in your arms the many small miracles
that die, and return each spring.
Yes, spring.
        Don't make me name all four seasons!
        For you, summer's just begun.

If I Can't Sleep

If I can't sleep, I can't write.
If I can't ease my son's pain, I can't sleep.
If I hadn't made love with my husband,
I wouldn't have given birth.
If I hadn't given birth, our son wouldn't be in pain.
If I hadn't been born among towering maples,
I wouldn't have tried to imitate growing things.
If I hadn't trusted trees, I wouldn't be so hurt by humans,
who aren't the same as trees, for when we suffer,
we want the world to suffer with us.
If I wasn't in pain, or full of joy, I couldn't write.
If I can't write, I can't sleep.

Call It Quits

If you're not a movie mogul, rock star, or President,
if you're not a CEO sitting on a billion in the bank,
no one will answer your e-mails, phone calls or letters.
You'll be helpless, hopeless, too old, too young,
in too much pain, the wrong color, some unacceptable
sex, a non-believer in some religion people kill for.
You could keep struggling to see through everyone's
skin to their slick, writhing guts, including your own.
Or, you could call it quits, and slip into the unknown,
inexhaustible, frothing teeth of the sea that turns us
all to brine, sweet salt of the universe.

Where Dreams Meet Daily Life

Sometimes I'm harsh with my family.
Beneath my harshness lie my tears.
Beneath my tears a woman filled with dreams,
who gave birth to words and children and gardens.

But now my children walk the earth
with bones that have finished growing,
and my husband reads the newspaper until I speak,
then answers and calls it love.

My words seem irrelevant, like my dreams,
crowded with strangers at loud parties
where I can't find anything to drink.
Did my dreams ripen because my rich life fed them?
Or did my hungry dreams feed my life?

The place where dreams meet daily life
must be blessed by what is unknown.
We move as a spirit flies, or as underground
water flows, the way stones still breathe
with the spirit that gave them birth.

Her Family

She's known them since she was born or they were born.
Some gave days and nights of reverie and their youthful arms to cradle her.
Others, silent, in pain, tried their best. A few seemed bent on destruction.
Some depended on her, and the more she gave the more they asked.
She wants to love them the way she loves the tangled family garden.
She wants to hold them as close as she holds her dreams.
She wants the awful grace of speaking eye to eye.
Yet each time she visits, she drives home with a half-eaten heart,
and peace descends upon her shoulders
as the racing pines and long, faithful fences lead her away.

White Wicker Chair With Wide Arms

Grandma sat here shelling sweet summer peas,
humming love songs and watching me dance
with the grace I always had when she was near.
Dad sat here, naked, reading the newspaper
and drinking a beer after digging the garden.
Mom relaxed here with her arms around our
sons, who smiled shyly the way children do
when someone older says things they cannot
fathom. She rested here again after her stroke,
rocking to heal herself. My husband and sons
lounge in the chair now, while we talk about
dinner or our dreams. I never sit in the chair
myself. I'd rather watch the people I love
safe in its welcoming arms.

for my mother, Maryanna Manfred

Grandma's Grave

Mother and I brush long drifts of snow from the gravestones
of my great grandfather and grandmother, great uncle and aunt,
two of mother's brothers, each less than a year old,
and her last-born brother, George Shorba, dead at sixteen:
> *1925 – 1942*
> *A Mastermind. My Beloved Son.*
But we can't find the grave of Grandma, who buried all the rest.

Mother stands dark-browed and musing, under the pines,
and I imagine her as a child, wondering why her mother
left home so often to tend the sick, the dying, the dead.
Borrowing a shovel, she digs, until she uncovers:
> *1889 – 1962*
> *Mary Shorba*

Mother almost never cries, but she does now. She stares
at this stone as if it were the answer to all the hidden things.

My Father-In-Law On The Phone

"All is quiet. All is new.
We don't even have weather anymore.
I open the paper and there's no news.
The television keeps playing repeats.
I have no more official positions.
The cat goes to sleep on my leg.
I pushed him away and he bit me.
You don't want to disturb a cat.
When you stand up, they start winding
in and out of your legs so you nearly fall.
Cats don't learn about these things.
They're nice though, I like them.
They're full of love for you.
That's all from here.
All is quiet.
All is new."

for Colonel Henry Popp, 90, WWII Veteran

Blue Mound, Luverne, Minnesota

> They say all is one instantaneously at any given moment:
> past, present, and future – so, if true, where is time...?
> > Frederick Manfred, Sr.

> You were not a house, not a home; but a sanctum,
> my refuge, an island of innocence.
> > Frederick Manfred, Jr.

Purple buffalo berries and yellow mullein bloom amid flowing grasses
and flesh-colored boulders tall as church steeples.
I was married here by Eagle Rock.
Before that I ran away to write poems.
Before that I dreamed of finding my future somewhere else
while a ring of black and white cows gathered to watch me sleep.
Before that settlers built sod huts and plowed fields of corn.
Before that Lakota braves ran buffalo off the quartzite cliffs for food.
Before that flower and grass seeds sprouted in the prairie winds.
I want to die looking out over these farms and fields,
by the old rocks and under the new sky.

ACKNOWLEDGMENTS AND FURTHER THANKS

I am grateful to the editors of the following publications for poems or versions of poems which originally appeared in them: "Rain On Water," "Swimming In The Rain," "Swimming Into Winter," *Stardust and Fate: The Blueroad Reader;* "My Father-In-Law On The Phone," "Swimming With A Hundred Year Old Snapping Turtle," *Sioux Falls Argus Leader*, June, 2007; "Swimming With A Hundred Year Old Snapping Turtle," Ted Kooser's National Newspaper Column, *American Life In Poetry*, August 2007.

Thanks to my sons, Ethan Rowan Pope and Nicholas Bly Pope, for their pencil drawings of snapping turtles. (www.popebrothersart.com)

I am immensely grateful to my husband, Tom Pope, for his editing help with these poems. Thanks also to Bly Pope, Rowan Pope, Robert Bly, Ruth Bly, and Scott King for their fine suggestions.